Recipe for Negotiating Business Deals Successfully

Dana L. Cradeur

Dana International Consulting, LLC
Post Box 9030
Jackson, WY 83002

Dana International Consulting, LLC
Post Box 9030
Jackson, WY 83002
Danaiconsulting.com
danaiconsulting@aol.com

Copyright © 2008 by Dana L. Cradeur

All rights reserved. No part of this book may be reproduced, stored in retrieval system, or transmitted in whole or in part, in any form or by any means, electronic, mechanical, photocopying, recording, or otherwise, without written permission from the author.

ISBN-13: 978-0-980-1277-4-4

Library of Congress Control Number: 2008902079

Printed in the United States of America.

The recipe card appearing on pages 4, 66 and in the appendix
Copyright © 2008 Dana L. Cradeur

Disclaimer

This book is designed to provide information on negotiating business deals. It is sold with the understanding that the publisher and author are not engaged in rendering legal, accounting, or other professional services. If legal or other expert assistance is required, the services of a competent professional should be sought.

This text should be used only as a general guide and not as the ultimate source of negotiation. The author and publisher shall have neither liability nor responsibility to any person or entity with respect to any loss or damage caused, or alleged to have been caused, directly or indirectly, by the information contained in this book.

Acknowledgments

I would like to thank all my friends and family who encouraged me in my new endeavor to write this book and to start my own business. I want to especially thank my friends (Roseline Chapel, Stacy Wilkins, Jessica Caldwell, Steve Pearce, and Melissa Cross) and my sister (Desiree LeBlanc) who believed in me and provided great ideas and feedback for my manuscript.

I sincerely thank Chef Robyne Befeld in Jackson Hole, WY for reviewing my manuscript, answering all my questions, offering creative ideas and providing productive feedback. I would like to express my appreciation to Chef John Wentworth, Banquet Chef, at the Spring Creek Ranch in Jackson Hole, WY for taking the time to answer all my questions about chefs in general and cooking chicken soup.

Table of Contents

CHAPTER 1: Cooking Up a Deal ... 1

CHAPTER 2: The Recipe - Negotiation Strategy ... 7
    I. Identifying the Ingredients ... 14
- Non-negotiable Item ... 15
- Assumption ... 17
- Constraint ... 18
- Concession ... 20
- Vendor List ... 24
- Buyer List ... 25
- Negotiation Scorecard ... 26
- Negotiating Abilities ... 27
- Competitors ... 30

    II. Analyzing the Ingredients ... 31
    III. Adding an Alternative Plan ... 32
    IV. Blending Integrity, Respect, Trust with Negotiating Abilities ... 33
    V. Developing a Negotiation Strategy ... 35
    VI. Negotiating ... 37
- Asking Key Questions ... 38
- Delivering Your Message ... 39
- Preparing for Your Negotiations ... 40

CHAPTER 3: Critical Success Factors — 43
- The Power of Emotions — 43
- Emotional Intelligence — 46
  - Attitude — 47
  - Managing Conflicts — 48
- Managing the Ego — 49
- Overcoming Fear — 52
- Patience — 53

CHAPTER 4: Closing the Deal — 55
- Finalizing an Agreement — 56
- Lessons Learned — 57

CHAPTER 5: Negotiating with Different Cultures — 59
- General and Business Mannerisms — 60
- Country Regimes — 64

CHAPTER 6: Negotiating Tips — 67

REFERENCES — 76
APPENDIX — 77
AFTERWORD — 80

Chapter 1

Cooking Up a Deal

When it comes to negotiating a successful business deal, how do you measure up? Do you know all of the components that go into negotiating and how to piece them together to determine the true value of the deal as well as the value you bring to the table? Do you have a set of techniques to help guide you through the process? When faced with a challenge like negotiating, people often search for guidelines or strategies to aid them in overcoming that challenge. We look for a roadmap to help us proceed—something that provides a simple overview and enables us to overcome difficult obstacles. We need a recipe.

Negotiation is a difficult process with complicated elements and facets. Having a recipe to negotiate provides you with the necessary guidelines to extract the most value from a deal along with having the other side satisfied with the terms and conditions of the deal. You need to understand the elements that are required to formulate your strategy, who you are negotiating with, and the culture you are negotiating in to negotiate effectively.

Think of negotiating a deal as you would cooking a meal. Without a well planned recipe, you run the risk of creating a disaster out of what may have been a delicious meal. "Cooking up" a successful deal without some guiding principles would be like cooking without a recipe except you risk more than a few displeased dinner guests. The most delicious meals often come from secret recipes, passed along in families or among friends. This book provides a secret recipe for negotiating successfully. The secret is in making negotiation simple and straightforward so that anyone can learn how to make profitable deals. Examples of the different types of deals where this technique can be applied are as follows:

- Buying/selling products or services
- Buying/selling/leasing real estate (commercial or residential)
- Buying/selling a business
- Investing in a capital venture
- Resolving a contractual dispute

Business negotiations can be very complex, and complex concepts often become simpler when we can make comparisons with something familiar. Take a chicken soup, for instance. Not many things in life are more familiar than that steamy bowl of comfort food. Cooking a pot of delicious chicken soup is a lot like negotiating a successful business deal. They both have a recipe, ingredients, and a desirable goal. Following are the key components for negotiating a deal that relates with cooking a chicken soup:

Chef	=	Negotiator
Recipe	=	Strategy
Pot	=	Culture
Ingredients	=	Elements of the Strategy
Cooking	=	Negotiating
Soup	=	The Deal
People Tasting the Soup	=	Counterparts in the Deal

A good chef has similar characteristics to a skilled negotiator. Some of these characteristics are good communication and listening skills, quick thinking, good record keeping, creativity, and multi-tasking skills. A good chef knows that the foundation for cooking a great pot of chicken soup is based on the quality of the ingredients and the type of pot used. Similarly, the foundation for a successful business strategy lies in the elements of the culture you are negotiating with and how you make an agreement come together. Different cultures require different negotiation strategies and tactics. Understanding the culture mannerism and regimes before negotiating any type of business deal is extremely important, just like understanding how the various types of pot materials (i.e., aluminum, cast iron, stainless steel, etc.) alter the way the soup is cooked. For the purpose of this book, the assumption is the chef will use a cast iron pot for cooking the chicken soup. This pot will represent negotiating within your culture. Chapter 5 will provide an overview of business and culture mannerisms and regimes that are critical to know prior to negotiating in a different culture.

Recipe for Negotiating Business Deals Successfully

When cooking chicken soup, the first thing a chef does is go over the list of ingredients. This recipe card in Figure 1 contains the key ingredients that make up the heart of the negotiation and chicken soup.

Figure 1

Imagine a chef has a large pot filled with every ingredient essential to cooking a delicious chicken soup. Each ingredient represents an important piece of the chicken soup, or in our case, the negotiation. The recipe will help you to extract the most value when cooking up your deal. You will understand how to add, subtract and blend or dilute each ingredient in order to create something of value.

A recipe for chicken soup requires you to spend time examining the ingredients to ensure the ingredients are fresh, not bruised, and satisfactory for making a mouth-watering chicken soup. Spoiled or unnecessary ingredients might cause the soup to have an unfavorable taste. Taking the time to investigate your negotiating ingredients will ensure that *your strategy* is strong, giving you an accurate picture of the business deal and the critical variables involved in closing a deal with precision and success.

Efficiency and a deliberate commitment to your goal are essential for both cooking and negotiating. For example, a clean and organized kitchen makes cooking easier and more enjoyable, just as beginning a negotiation with an organized plan will help you to complete the task set before you with greater ease. The amount of information you must remember and maintain to negotiate successfully can be cumbersome at times and easy to forget. This book provides templates to aid you in organizing your information since negotiations center on the accurate exchange of information.

Just like the secret to cooking a delicious pot of chicken soup lies in its simplicity and the key essentials, the secret to understanding negotiation

Recipe for Negotiating Business Deals Successfully

is in making it simple and understanding the fundamentals. In the next chapters, you will explore the recipe for negotiation; the critical success factors; how to close a profitable deal; information on negotiating with different cultures; and finally, some general tips for negotiating. As you read, remember that anyone can become a successful negotiator with the right tools, the confidence to succeed, and a willingness to learn and grow through continued practice and understanding. Gather your ingredients, investigate and test, develop your plan, take action, and enjoy!

Chapter 2

The Recipe: The Negotiation Strategy

Building relationships is the fundamental component in seeking potential business opportunities. As opportunities are discussed within relationships, identify and determine whether those opportunities are worth pursuing by seeking the proper information in order to understand all the variables of the deal. If you believe that the opportunity is viable, this is the time to start formulating a strategy. You may search for different types of negotiation strategies/tactics from various sources (i.e., negotiation books, internet, colleagues, etc.) in the same way you would seek recipes from various sources (i.e., cookbooks, internet, friends, etc.). When seeking the proper negotiation strategy for your deal, it is important to investigate and pay close attention to the elements that formulate the strategy, just as you would the ingredients in a recipe. Remember, not *all* recipes lead to an extraordinary soup.

As a chef, the ultimate goal is to cook a chicken soup with a flavor that is pleasing to all. As a negotiator, the goal is to create an agreement in which both parties are mutually satisfied. As stated earlier, the recipe represents the strategy to achieve that goal. Capturing all the elements of the deal will enable you to develop an effective negotiation strategy. Think of negotiating in the same way that you might think of *cooking* chicken soup. With the right ingredients, mixture, and proper blend, you can produce an extraordinary chicken soup or close a lucrative deal and have the other party content with the agreement every time. By comparing the recipe for negotiating a deal with this recipe for chicken soup, you can easily understand how to cook up the perfect deal.

Recipe for Negotiating a Business Deal (*Chicken Soup*)

Ingredients
Non-negotiables *(Carrots)*, Assumptions *(Tomatoes)*, Constraints *(Zucchini)*, Concession List *(Chicken)*, Competitors *(Onions)*, Negotiating Ability *(Seasoning)*

Analyze
Yours and The Other Side's Ingredients

Mix
(Carrots, Tomatoes, Zucchinis, Chicken, Onions)

Add
Alternative Plan *(Beef)*

Blend
Integrity, Trust, Respect *(Water)*
with
Enthusiasm, Emotional Intelligence, Positive Attitude,
Good Communication and Listening Skills,
Patience *(Seasoning)*

Negotiate (*Cook*)
Extracting the Most Value *(Creating a Delicious Taste)*

The Recipe: The Negotiation Strategy

A successful negotiator must investigate and document the key ingredients of a business deal, just as a good chef must understand and value each ingredient in the soup. The ingredients of a negotiation are the **non-negotiable items, assumptions, constraints, concession lists, negotiating abilities,** and **competitors (alternatives)**. Investigating and documenting these ingredients provide you with a clear understanding of your options and the value you bring to the negotiation table. Without some of these key ingredients, your strategy will be haphazard, and you could risk failure.

Analyzing your negotiating ingredients is like mixing the ingredients in chicken soup. An alternative plan allows you to have options when your counterpart does not agree with the terms of your deal. Blending integrity, respect, and trust is essential in being a reputable negotiator, just like adding water is essential in making the chicken soup. The seasoning for the chicken soup requires constant monitoring, tasting, and adjusting as the soup is being prepared, just like each side's different negotiating abilities require constant monitoring and adjusting as the negotiation progresses in order to achieve a desirable goal. Finally, cooking the soup represents the actual negotiation.

A strong negotiating strategy along with good negotiating skills brings tenacity and power to the table. By being well prepared, you are able to handle surprises and alter your strategic direction when necessary. The key is to leverage your position so that you orchestrate the terms of the path forward and the structure of the deal.

A negotiation has many facets that change the dynamics of how the deal plays out. To understand these facets, you need to know which ingredients are considered negotiable items and what ingredients are considered influencers in the negotiation. The illustration of the chicken and vegetable soup shown in Figure 2.1 displays the ingredients ranking from non-negotiable to negotiable. The seasoning and onion represent the ingredients that directly influence the negotiation.

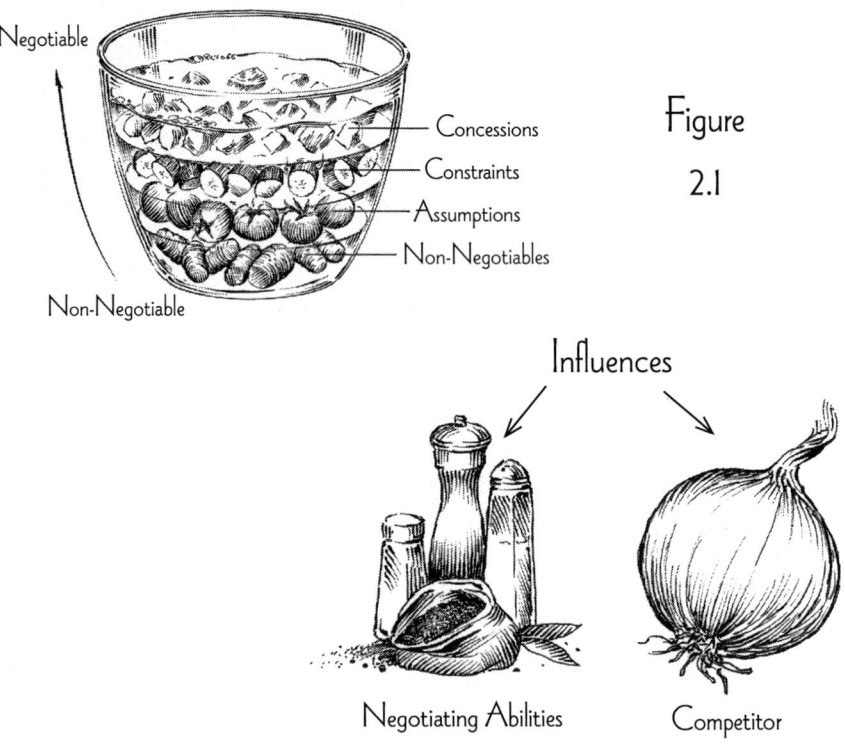

Figure 2.1

The Recipe: The Negotiation Strategy

The way the negotiable items are divided in the bowl will help you understand how easily one ingredient could transform and change the requirements of the negotiation. Unlike the foods used in cooking, some negotiation ingredients have a special ability to morph into other ingredients during the negotiating process. For example, you might plan to manufacture a product in a foreign country whose currency is much lower than the US. One of your assumptions might be that the US dollar will remain strong within the next several years but before the deal is completed, the US dollar plunges and the foreign country currency gains strength against it. Your assumption just turned into a major constraint, because the devaluation of the dollar affects your profit level and it may no longer be advantageous to manufacture your product in that country. You may have to rethink your strategy or decide whether the deal is still worth pursuing.

The soup bowl with its ingredients represents your negotiable scale starting with the non-negotiables. Your non-negotiables are the items you consider to be unchanging and never up for discussion; in other words, they are your deal breakers. The next ingredient in the soup bowl represents your assumptions. Assumptions are anything that you believe could be true about the other side, a situation, or the deal. (Assumptions may or may not have an impact on the deal.) When an assumption changes the direction of the deal or has an impact on the deal if proven true, then the assumption will move up or down the negotiable scale, and morph into a new ingredient. The assumption could become a deal breaker, constraint, or concession, all of which introduce new variables into the negotiation arena and change the make-up of the deal.

A constraint can be a restriction, limitation, potential risk, and/or liability with possible financial and/or contractual implications if not resolved or mitigated properly. A constraint may or may not have a significant effect on the deal. If a constraint has substantial risk, then it could turn out to be a deal breaker. Whatever the case is, a constraint, like an assumption, can often change to represent a new variable in the negotiation.

Concessions are any items, services, and/or locations that are considered negotiable. A negotiable item usually remains a concession unless an unforeseen event takes place that moves it down on the negotiable scale. One example of this is when a manufacturing company sells a particular item that takes one month to produce and an unforeseen steel strike occurs. The steel required to build the product is now unavailable; therefore, the delivery time becomes unknown. The buyer needs the steel delivered within two months. This situation could easily cause the concession to move down the negotiable scale to change into a constraint or deal breaker. The owner may be able to mitigate the risk of losing the deal by buying the steel at a much higher price from another company. In this situation, the concession will change into another ingredient, due to implications of securing the steel, which in turn could change the terms of the deal.

The soup bowl is a simple methodology to assist you in remembering the type of negotiable ingredients required in a negotiation and how they can manipulate the negotiation process. The seasoning and the onion next to the bowl represent yours and the other side's negotiating abilities, as well as the abilities of your competitors. The flavor of a soup

The Recipe: The Negotiation Strategy

can change dramatically by the amount of onions and seasoning put into the soup, just like your negotiating abilities and competitors can have a major impact on how you communicate, negotiate, and structure the deal. How you communicate the deal will influence how receptive the other side will be to your terms and conditions. This is similar to how a chef would describe his soup on a menu. Negotiating abilities are comprised of many skill sets, all which will be discussed in detail later in this chapter.

How your competitors position themselves or, more generally, your opponent's alternatives will determine how you structure the deal and communicate your position to the other side. Yours and the other side's negotiating abilities, along with your competitor's, introduce all types of variables that can cause the negotiation to be very complex and cumbersome.

All these ingredients play a key role in gathering all the components that make up and surround the deal so that you can build a powerful negotiation strategy. Before developing your strategy, you must first gather and document your ingredients in a well organized manner. By being unorganized, you potentially overlook critical information that could put the negotiation in jeopardy. Keeping pieces of information on your computer, on a note pad, on a business card, or on a napkin is symptomatic of disorganization. They become easy to forget or misplace. If your information is in numerous places, how are you able to see the overall picture and accurately assess the negotiation? By being disorganized, you may lose information and put yourself at a disadvantage. The statement *"One who keeps good records usually wins,"* in George H.

Ross' book *Trump Style Negotiation* is worth testing so that you can reap the benefits (pg 148).

This chapter will assist you in organizing your information by providing examples of templates to capture each of your ingredients. The templates are the groundwork of your recipe for negotiation. When using the templates, you should first evaluate the deal and determine how much information is required to be documented. To keep this exercise simple and easy, start by creating a spreadsheet with one or more worksheets to capture the appropriate ingredients. *Figure 2.2* lists all the ingredients required to develop a highly effective strategy.

	Goal - Profitable Deal (Chicken Soup)
Non-Negotiables	Assumptions	Constraints	Concession Lists	Other Side Negotiating Ability	Competitors
Carrots	Tomatoes	Zucchini	Chicken	Seasoning	Onions

Figure 2.2

I. Identifying the Ingredients

The ingredients have three main functions: 1) to determine the true value of the deal; 2) to determine the true value you bring to the deal; and 3) to assist in formulating strategies to extract the most value. The ingredients make up the foundation of your strategy. Without the ingredients or with poor quality ingredients, your negotiation strategy will be weak or non-existent. Investigating and documenting the ingredients are what most negotiators spend the least amount of time doing since these tasks are time consuming. By doing your homework, you will have

The Recipe: The Negotiation Strategy

a distinct advantage in the negotiation, since you will have a clear picture of what the deal truly offers and the constraints surrounding the deal. By identifying and updating your ingredients, you will always know where you stand in the negotiation and whether or not the deal is still worth pursuing.

Negotiating business deals can be very time consuming and expensive so why not invest upfront to help you determine whether each deal has the value you seek with workable constraints? In the end, the constraints may out-weigh the value, but you will never know unless you investigate thoroughly. Your up-front investment includes time spent in investigating your ingredients and in seeking legal, accounting, and financial advice to ensure you have covered all your exposed risks. Take the time to work through each facet of a negotiation before you begin to negotiate. Now it is time to understand the role each of the ingredients plays in the negotiation: **non-negotiable items, constraints, assumptions, concession lists, the other side's negotiating ability, and competitors (alternatives).**

1. Non-negotiable Item

A non-negotiable item represents the carrot in the chicken soup. A carrot is firm and nonflexible when raw, but it softens through the cooking process. In a negotiation, the non-negotiable items are firm and nonflexible just like carrots. **Non-negotiable items are any commercial and/or contractual terms and conditions that must be adhered to in order to proceed with the deal.** For example, you have been looking for months to lease a townhouse to live in and you finally come across the perfect place. While reading the lease contract, you notice several terms that require modifications and/or need to be removed. One of the terms you wish to be removed is a sales clause. This clause stated that the owner has the right to sell the townhouse at anytime during the year of your lease and you have to ensure that the townhouse is presentable whenever a potential buyer comes to view the house. Well, you are surprised to discover this sales clause because the owner never mentioned about selling the townhouse. You discuss removing the clause with the owner, but s/he is adamant about not changing the contract. At this time, you have to decide if this clause is a non-negotiable item for you. In other words, is it a deal breaker? If you choose to accept the sales clause, then the negotiation can proceed. Like a firm carrot, non-negotiable items get softer because they are no longer a threat in the negotiation.

As soon as possible in the negotiation process, define your non-negotiable items and try to uncover the other side's non-negotiable items by asking direct or indirect questions. If the non-negotiable terms and conditions cannot be met, then there is no deal to be established. Spend time defining your non-negotiable items before the negotiation process begins, so that no time and money are wasted in negotiating items that are not negotiable. *Figure 2.3* is an example of how to capture yours and the other side's non-negotiable items.

Non-Negotiables (Carrots)	
Your Non-Negotiables	Other Side's Non-Negotiables

Figure 2.3

2. Assumption

An assumption represents the tomato in the chicken soup because a tomato is soft, juicy, and it dissolves when cooked. **An assumption can be anything that you believe may be true about the other side, a situation, or the deal.** Realize that assumptions are not facts until proven so; in other words, assumptions will turn into another element just like tomatoes when cooked long enough dissolve into the chicken broth. Assumptions could lead you down the wrong path if not tested carefully. Test all assumptions by asking probing questions and listening carefully to determine whether your assumptions are correct (Ross, pg. 36).

For example, you are a vendor and a critical factor for your client is delivery time. You assume that you can meet their deadline but it will be tight. You also assume that the client will afford you a certain amount of leeway if you push the deadline back. The deal moves forward and you submit the contract. Before signing, the client inserts a clause stating a substantial penalty if the delivery deadline is not met. Your assumption that there would not be a penalty for a late delivery time has put you in a bind. You are not sure that you can actually meet this deadline and now the deal has come to a halt. You must now make the decision as to whether you will risk paying a penalty or let go of the deal. Your assumption just transformed into a constraint or deal breaker.

List all your assumptions and test them throughout the negotiation process. By testing your assumptions, you reduce your risk and gain better understanding of the other side's terms, conditions, constraints,

Recipe for Negotiating Business Deals Successfully

and interests. Too many people make assumptions and are afraid to verify whether they are correct. This kind of fear can cause you to make precarious decisions which could lead to financial or contractual consequences.

In order to test your assumptions, take the appropriate time to prepare questions to ensure you obtain the information you are seeking. If the other side chooses not to disclose the information, try asking indirect questions about the subject matter or finding other resources to obtain the validation of your assumptions. *Figure 2.4* is an example of how to track your assumptions.

Assumptions (Tomatoes)		
Assumptions	Tested (Yes/No)	Date Confirmed

Figure 2.4

3. Constraint

A constraint represents the zucchini in the chicken soup because both have similar characteristics. A fresh zucchini has a strange way of being somewhat firm yet slightly flexible before cooking; yet it softens as it cooks. Constraints can be soft, flexible, or firm (deal breakers). Firm constraints may appear to threaten the deal, but with workable solutions the constraints become flexible and soften when mitigated. Constraints can stop a deal from moving forward by exposing you or your company to potential risks and/or liabilities that are financially unfeasible to mitigate or there is no possible solution for mitigation. **A constraint can be a restriction, limitation, potential risk, and/or liability with possible financial and/or contractual implications if not resolved or mitigated properly.** Conduct a thorough investigation and seek legal, accounting and financial advice to identify all risks and liabilities, so that no surprises occur once the agreement or contract has been signed.

One example of a major risk with a financial liability is buying an existing building in an unfamiliar area and not having the soil inspected for environmental toxins. A year later the environmental department decides to conduct a soil inspection around your building and the soil tests positive for toxins. Well, guess who pays to remove the toxins? You do; and the cost to remove the toxins could be in the millions. If a soil inspection was performed during your investigation period, the owner of the property would have been responsible for cleaning up the toxic soil instead of you.

Throughout the negotiation, identify and document yours and the other side's constraints. Assign a risk level of high, medium, or low to each constraint. For your medium to high risk constraints, a mitigation plan is recommended to determine if the risk or liability can be reduced or eliminated. Exposed risk or liability could cost you millions of dollars if not identified and resolved or mitigated during the negotiation. By documenting the other side's constraints, you will know at all times if the deal could be in jeopardy due to a potential risk or liability. Depending upon how important this deal is to you, you may wish to assist them in coming up with solutions to mitigate their risk that could hinder the deal.

Figure 2.5 is an example of a simple way to capture and monitor your and the other side's constraints. You may wish to add a dollar amount to each constraint to determine if the constraint is a deal breaker.

Constraints (Zucchini)			
Constraints	Risk (High/Med/Low)	Mitigation Plan	Other Side's Constraints	Risk (High/Med/Low)

Figure 2.5

4. Concession

A concession represents the chicken broth and chicken. The chicken is the substance of the soup just as concessions are the substance of the deal. Without the chicken and the broth there would be no chicken soup, and without the concessions there would be no negotiation. **A concession is any item, service, and/or location that is considered negotiable.** Your concession list enables you to learn how easily money slips through your fingers, which can be very costly to you. This list is one of the most critical elements in the negotiation and represents items to be traded.

The Recipe: The Negotiation Strategy

Here are some examples of concessions:

- Price
- Leasing vs. Buying
- Costs
- Quality
- Market Value
- Demand
- Time
- Service
- Margin
- Contractual Terms and Conditions
- Location

Remember, everything is negotiable with the exception of the non-negotiable items. The more value you place on an item the less negotiable the item becomes. By listing your concessions and placing a value on each, you will have a better understanding of what you might trade in return for an item of greater value. For the items on which you place a medium to high value, it would behoove you to determine how flexible you are with the terms and/or conditions and how much leeway you have for negotiating each of these concessions. To have a clear appreciation of your flexibility and negotiation range, list all your medium to high concessions and state the terms and/or conditions to be presented, the range of acceptance, and what is unacceptable or a deal breaker for each concession. *Figure 2.6A* is an example of a vendor's terms and conditions assessment.

Concession	Vendor's Terms and Conditions		
	Present to the Other Side	Goal	Unacceptable or Deal Breaker
Price	$300K	$300K - $270K	$230K or Less
Delivery Time	6 Months	6 - 5 Months	4 Months or Less
Consulting Srvcs. ☐ of People	8 - 6 Resources	8 - 4 Resources	2 Resources or Fewer
Margin		30 - 20%	5% or Less
Payment Terms	30 Days	30 - 60 Days	90 Days

Figure 2.6A

Documenting your terms and conditions as shown in *Figure 2.6A* allows you to stay focused so that you can maintain a profitable deal and will not be inclined to give away too much of your value.

A deal breaker is a concession with terms and/or conditions that you feel impedes the deal to the point that the deal is not worth pursuing. Examples of deal breakers are when the deal becomes economically unfeasible, the financial and/or liability risks are too high, there are legal issues, or there is a problem with the scheduled delivery time. A concession with an unacceptable term may not always be a deal breaker, because when you evaluate the entire deal, the unacceptable term's value is not enough to stop the deal from moving forward. An example of an unacceptable term that may not be considered a deal breaker could be payment terms. Your goal is to have 30 to 60 days payment terms, but the other side requires 90 days. Though 90 days is considered unacceptable, you might still consider accepting the term, because the rest of the deal is very attractive.

The Recipe: The Negotiation Strategy

Make sure you account for all financial and contractual risk potential for all concessions. Some people tend to overlook the significance of identifying their unacceptable terms or deal breakers and sticking to them. By not identifying what is unacceptable or a deal breaker for each of your concessions, you may discount too much of your value, pay too much, or be exposed to unnecessary risks.

By conducting a terms and conditions assessment, you are then able to know the precise boundaries in which you can negotiate. This makes negotiating easier when negotiations are multifaceted, because you have a clear understanding of the range you can negotiate for each concession. The more prepared you are in knowing the implications of your concession terms and conditions, the more confidence you will have in making astute business decisions. This knowledge will enable you to create solutions to work around concessions hindering the deal.

You want to identify your concession list as well as understand the other side's. Knowing the other side's list provides pertinent information about their motivations, interests, constraints, and the value they place on certain items. In negotiating business deals, you will either represent the vendor — the person selling a product, service, or business — or the buyer. To assist you in determining the type of information your concession list should capture, *Figures 2.6B & C* represent the vendor and the buyer's concession list. At the end of the negotiation, it is important for you to understand how well you negotiated and what areas require improvements. A good method to use is the negotiation scorecard which is shown in Figure *2.6D*.

Vendor List

The vendor table, Figure 2.6B, consists of a concession list and the terms and conditions assessment. The concession's list provides information on standard concessions, concessions to be traded, and the value the concessions bring to each side. A vendor's standard concessions are products and services offered to the client at no additional cost. Here are some examples of standard concessions:

- Entertainment (Golfing, hunting, fishing, sporting events and opera tickets)
- 1 to 2 days of free engineering services
- Free delivery
- Guarantees
- 30-day software evaluation license
- 1 to 2 days of free consultation
- 1 to 2 days of free training
- Standard discounts

By comparing the standard concessions with the concessions to be traded, you can then determine if you are giving away or trading value. These two concession lists next to each other will help you to stay focused on the value you can extract from the deal. When the other side asks you for a particular concession, try not to trade your concessions too quickly, because you start diminishing the value of your service or product.

The Recipe: The Negotiation Strategy

Vendor							
Concession List (Chicken)				Terms and Conditions			
Priority	Standard Concession	Concessions to Trade	Value to the Other Side (High, Med, Low $)	Value to You (High, Med, Low $)	T&C to Present to the Other Side	Goal	Unacceptable T&C or Deal Breaker

Figure 2.6B

Buyer List

The buyer's table, *Figure 2.6C*, consists of a concession list and the terms and conditions assessment. The concession list provides concessions to be traded and the value they bring to each party. By capturing both parties' concession list, you gain greater insight into understanding the other side's interests, issues, and motivations. The more knowledge you obtain about the other side, the more you are able to communicate and influence the direction of the negotiation and create an agreement in which both parties are mutually satisfied.

Buyer						
Concession List (Chicken)				Terms and Conditions		
Priority	Concessions to Trade	Value to the Other Side (High, Med, Low $)	Value to You (High, Med, Low $)	T&C to Present to the Other Side	Goal	Unacceptable T&C or Deal Breaker

Figure 2.6C

Negotiation Scorecard

Your concession list at the end of the deal is your scorecard on how well you and your team negotiated. Your scorecard will disclose how lucrative the deal was for you and how much money was left on the table or given away. With this scorecard, you may learn that you have been giving away too much value and receiving very little in return. Unfortunately, this situation occurs quite frequently, especially when you do not take the time to gain the proper knowledge to understand all the variables in the negotiation. *Figure 2.6D* represents an example of a negotiation scorecard.

	Negotiation Scorecard			
Item No.	What Have You Actually Traded or Given Away?	$ Value Given to the Other Side (Revenue Loss)	What Has the Other Side Given to You?	Value to You in $ (High, Medium, Low)

Figure 2.6D

One common scenario is giving away too much value in hopes that a contract will be signed more quickly. Would you sign a contract with no compelling reason, especially if you believe that someone was giving away his value for free? How much value have you given away without asking for anything in return in hopes that a contract would be signed quickly? When this happens, does the other side sign the contract? If so, how long does it take and what compelled the other side to sign? This

The Recipe: The Negotiation Strategy

situation is similar to ordering a chicken soup along with one or more entrees for the price of only the chicken soup. Your restaurant will not be able to stay in business if you give away additional entrees for the price of one. These are important questions to ask in order to start maximizing your value and learning new ways to negotiate better deals. Once you start identifying and tracking the concession lists, you will find it harder to give away value without asking for something in return.

5. Negotiating Abilities

Negotiating abilities represent the seasoning in the chicken soup. In negotiating, you are constantly adjusting your abilities and emotions to resolve issues and to create a workable agreement. When seasoning the chicken soup, the chef is constantly adding and adjusting the seasoning based on his taste, perception of the consumer, and his experience so that the soup has just the right flavor.

A good negotiator will adapt certain abilities to accommodate the other side into a mutually desirable agreement. A negotiator may have a variety of abilities, just as chicken soup can have a variety of seasoning. Different people have different abilities — accomplished negotiators often have many. Experienced negotiators possess inner strength, emotional intelligence, good communication and listening skills, positive attitudes, creativity, and open minds. In addition to possessing these interpersonal skills, a negotiator needs to be an investigator, team player, strategist, quick thinker, and a good record keeper. As you can see, seasoned negotiators acquire a variety of skill sets that enable them to consistently close profitable deals.

Recipe for Negotiating Business Deals Successfully

People's emotions play a major role in negotiation. Understanding the dynamics of emotions and how emotions influence the deal is critical. Emotions can produce a very profitable deal in negotiation, but they can also cause the deal to stall or cause you to get burned. Different types of emotions influence different types of outcomes just like the amount of seasoning you put in a chicken soup changes the soup's flavor. A chef will "add seasoning in small amounts tasting after each addition" to ensure the soup's flavor is in balance (Chef Robyne Befeld). When negotiating you should always be aware of how your emotions are affecting the negotiation and adjust your emotions accordingly if they are inhibiting the deal from moving forward.

Spend time getting to know the other side's behavior and negotiating ability so that you are well prepared to deal with any tactics the other side may initiate. When you are investigating or negotiating, remember people like to be acknowledged for their ideas, solutions, or proposals. We all like to feel that our ideas are valuable. Make a special effort to let the other side know that you heard or understood their point of view. By acknowledging the other side's ideas, you help create an amiable negotiation.

A good chef always listens to what people say about her food so she can perfect it. Good listening skills are most important during negotiating after your strategy is formulated. Fine tune your listening skills by hearing what people say instead of using their talk time to plan what you will say next. If you listen to what the other side is saying, they will be more open to sharing information. The more information the other side shares with you, the more you understand their needs, constraints, and tactics, making it easier for you to handle surprises or obstacles that arise.

The Recipe: The Negotiation Strategy

A positive attitude along with enthusiasm entices the other side to become interested in what you have to offer. The other side will feel your excitement, which allures them into wanting to hear what you have to say and work with you. Creating a positive and friendly atmosphere allows people to relax. Communication becomes more open and trusting. The more knowledge you uncover about the other side, the more you are able to communicate more clearly as to how to establish a workable agreement. Keep in mind that having flexibility and an open mind fosters creativity and innovative solutions.

Understanding the other side's negotiating abilities is a key ingredient in developing your negotiation strategy and tactics. *Figure 2.7* is an example of the type of information you should obtain about the other side (Ross, pg 133). The more knowledge you acquire about the other side, the more you are able to out-maneuver their tactics, and the more confidence you possess in the negotiation room.

Other Side Negotiating Ability (Seasoning)								
Names	Emotions Displayed (Calm, Pleasant, Aggressive, Angry, Others)	Tactics Used in Negotiating	Trustworthy (Yes/No)	Decision Maker (Yes/No)	Track Record (Good, Avg, Poor, Unknown)	Subject Matter Expert (Yes/Somewhat/No/Unknown)	Decision Required Soon (Yes/No)	Complaints

Figure 2.7

6. Competitor

A competitor represents the onion in the chicken soup, because just like chopping an onion, a competitor can make you cry. When cooking your soup, you gauge the amount of onions you put in your soup just as you would gauge the next move your competitors will make. Too many onions in your soup can cause the taste to change in the same way that too many competitors in the market can change the terms and conditions of your deal. The way in which your competitor(s) negotiate against you is significant in determining the direction of your strategy and how you will structure the deal.

In order to see the overall picture of what your competitors are doing and the tactics used against you in negotiating, you must track as much information as possible. Some general information to investigate about your competition includes pricing, constraints pertaining to the deal, motives for pursuing the deal, and concessions they are willing to give away or trade. As new information unfolds, update your competitor spreadsheet and modify your negotiation strategy if necessary.

| Competitor (Onions) ||||||
Competitor	Price	Deal Constraints	Motives	Concessions They are Willing to Give Away or Trade

Figure 2.8

The Recipe: The Negotiation Strategy

You are now ready to investigate and document ingredients for each side. To assist you in organizing and maintaining your information, the ingredients have been grouped into three worksheets and are provided in Appendix A:

Worksheet 1
- Non-negotiable Items
- Assumptions
- Constraints

Worksheet 2
- Vendor Concession Lists and Terms and Conditions
- Buyer Concession Lists and Terms and Conditions
- Negotiation Scorecard

Worksheet 3
- Other Side Negotiating Ability
- Competitors

II. Analyzing the Ingredients

Analyzing the negotiating ingredients is just as critical as properly mixing the ingredients for the chicken soup. Both of these steps are essential in achieving your goal. Reviewing and analyzing your negotiating ingredients enables you to understand the true value of the deal in order assist you in developing a strategy for negotiating the best deal possible, just as properly mixing the right ingredients in chicken soup makes a delicious and comforting soup every time.

Analyzing the ingredients allows you to identify the critical variables of and obtain an understanding of the value you bring to the deal in order to structure your terms and conditions. The ingredients are the foundation of your strategy. Without the ingredients, you will not be able to determine an accurate direction for how to proceed in the negotiation.

III. Adding an Alternative Plan

An alternative plan provides options for both parties. A chef must be somewhat flexible with her menu. If the menu only has chicken soup and the chef's customer calls in advance to inform the chef that she is allergic to poultry but loves beef the chef must be able to accommodate the customer. To be accommodating, the chef will substitute beef for the chicken. By the chef's being flexible and planning ahead, the customer will be able to enjoy a delicious bowl of beef soup and her experience at the restaurant will turn out to be gratifying.

As a negotiator, an alternative plan is crucial because it allows for another option if an agreement cannot be met, flexibility in the negotiation, and the ability to make intelligent decisions regarding how to proceed with the deal. Business negotiations are about strategizing to optimize your position in influencing the other side to an agreeable contract. Always consider having an alternative plan to your strategy. An alternative plan should be identified at the beginning of the negotiation instead of waiting until you encounter a problem. Having an alternative plan allows you to enter the negotiation with confidence and power, because you will not feel pressured to make a deal unless it is right for you.

The Recipe: The Negotiation Strategy

Sometimes the best alternative plan is to simply walk away from an undesirable deal. Without an alternative plan, people tend to feel more pressure causing them to secure an unprofitable deal (particularly when the deal is worth a large sum of money). When this occurs, people lose sight of profitability along with the value they bring to the table and may focus on closing the deal in any way possible, which only engenders bad contracts for you or your company.

Use your knowledge of negotiation to your advantage. Try to find out if the other side has an alternative plan by asking indirect questions. If you are not able to determine if they have a plan, then ask them directly. They may not tell you but at least you tried. If the other side has no alternative plan, then they could be pressured to make a deal. This information strengthens your position in the negotiation. If the other side does have an alternative plan, it is vital that you have one as well.

IV. Blending Integrity, Respect, Trust with Negotiating Abilities

Negotiation is more about gaining respect from the other side than making the other side your friend. You want to create a relationship based on respect, integrity, and trust. You are not there to make a new buddy, you are there to make a business deal. There may be times when the other side is not pleased with the terms you present; but remember not to take it personally. Conflicting ideas make it possible for each side to recognize the other's perspective. Healthy conflict is difficult to come by without a certain amount of trust. This means that unless there is trust in a relationship, people often shy away from bringing up conflict because they are afraid the relationship will not withstand it. Think of a new dating relationship compared to a marriage. A married couple can have a big argument over finances. The relationship will usually sustain the argument, oftentimes creating a new shared perspective on the original issue. Conversely, individuals who have just initiated their romantic relationship may internalize dissenting issues because they do not trust each other enough to have a major disagreement.

Trust is essential in a negotiation and can grow out of mutual respect. Respecting another person is not about affinity or judging whether someone is right or wrong. Rather, respect stems from recognizing the humanity and complexity in others and extending that recognition into the relationship. The Golden Rule is often cited as the foundation for respect: treat others as you would like to be treated. Realize, though, that the Golden Rule contains a hidden assumption. The assumption is that you respect yourself enough to warrant fair and positive treatment from others. Therefore, you should remember another well known rule: *in respecting another, you must respect yourself.*

Respecting yourself leads to the most important virtue in business: integrity. Integrity comes from doing what you say you are going to do, doing it well, and doing it on time. In a book about Donald Trump's negotiating ability, George H. Ross states that "the other side will pay a premium for peace of mind and confidence in your integrity" (pg. 30).

The water for the chicken soup represents integrity, respect, and trust because water is essential in creating the soup. Without the water, you have no soup. Integrity, respect, and trust are essential in closing any deal if you wish to be known as a reputable and successful negotiator.

How you blend your negotiating abilities into the negotiation is critical. Negotiation requires that you blend into whatever business environment you encounter. You want the other side to feel comfortable and at ease around you. If the other side is formal, you need to be formal. If they dress casually, you dress casually, but avoid being too casual. You are not there to intimidate the other side. If you intimidate the other side, they will close off emotionally and will not feel at ease in disclosing information, which will hinder the negotiation. Negotiating requires you to be accustomed to juggling multiple skills and evaluating your emotions so that they stay under control, like monitoring the seasoning of your chicken soup. If you blend in too much seasoning, your soup will be too spicy for some people to enjoy. Your goal is for people to enjoy eating your soup, so it is important to blend the seasoning just right.

> **Once you have documented and analyzed your negotiation ingredients, you are now ready to develop a POWERFUL negotiation strategy.**

V. Developing a Negotiation Strategy

As mentioned earlier, the recipe represents your negotiation strategy. Like the recipe for chicken soup, the negotiation recipe informs you what ingredients are required to develop the roadmap that will assist you in achieving your results. To develop an effective strategy, you must have a thorough understanding of the overall picture as well as all the constraints and critical variables of the deal. Here are some questions to assist you in developing your strategy:

- What are the key steps to accomplishing your goal?
- What is the true value of the deal?
- What are your top 3 - 5 concessions you will consider trading if required?
- What are your top 3 - 5 concessions you prefer not to trade?
- What are the terms and conditions you plan to offer?
- What is your timeframe in closing the deal?
- What is the other side's timeframe in closing the deal?
- How will you structure the deal?
- How will you present your offer?
- What message do you wish to deliver?
- How do you think the other side will react to your offer?
- Who is on your negotiation team?
- Who is the lead negotiator?

Once you define your strategy, think about the tactics required to achieve that strategy. *Figure 2.9* is an example of how to document and monitor your strategy and tactics. During the negotiation, your strategy may move in a new direction due to an unforeseen change or development. Updating your strategy will enable you to maintain focus in the future just as updating a recipe helps you to perfect your chicken soup.

The Recipe: The Negotiation Strategy

Date	Strategy	Still Valid (Yes/No)	Changes	Tactics

Figure 2.9

VI. Negotiating – Extracting the Most Value
(Cooking - Creating a Delicious Taste)

Now you should recognize the importance of every ingredient in the recipe for negotiation. Uncovering, documenting, and analyzing the right ingredients along with developing a powerful strategy are key if you want to negotiate successfully. As a negotiator, your role is to extract the most value from the deal while having the other side satisfied with the agreement. Similarly, when a chef cooks a chicken soup, her role is to make a profit on her chicken soup as well as create a delicious soup for people to enjoy eating.

Negotiations have no rules or restrictions regarding *how* to negotiate, so it is important to maintain some skepticism about what the other side discloses throughout the negotiation until the contract is signed *(Ross, pg. 3)*. Negotiation is about how well you play the game. If you are proactive, flexible, and open minded, you will stay ahead of the game by knowing when to adjust the terms and conditions of the deal and being open to creative solutions that will work for both parties.

Negotiations are about acquiring knowledge and how to use that knowledge to manage the direction of the negotiation. By recognizing that knowledge equals power in negotiations, you can leverage yourself by asking key questions, communicating a persuasive offering and being properly prepared for the negotiation.

Asking Key Questions

Everyone knows that questions are crucial in obtaining information during a negotiation. Here are several major points to think about before and during the negotiation.

Point #1

Take the appropriate amount of time to think about the types of questions you wish to ask and how to ask them. Negotiations can be very time consuming, and time truly is money, so spend adequate time preparing your questions.

Point #2

Never be afraid of asking tough questions, especially when you feel uncomfortable in asking. Questions regarding your assumptions or events that could jeopardize the deal might make you feel uncomfortable, but no matter how uncomfortable you are, you should always verify them. Not verifying your assumptions could cause serious problems in the negotiation. Confirming if a deal is in jeopardy is crucial in order for you to determine if it is still worth pursuing; otherwise, new terms may be required to complete the deal. By being proactive and asking tough questions, you obtain vital information, get a head start in finding workable solutions to problems, and stay ahead of your competitors.

Point #3

Never fear a negative response from the other side when you are offering specific terms. Words like "no" provide the opportunity to work through roadblocks, because it allows you to gain insight into the other side's concerns and constraints regarding what you are offering. The more information you uncover, the more you are able to analyze the situation and determine the feasibility of the deal. If the deal is worth moving forward, the knowledge you obtain will be valuable in crafting an agreeable deal.

Delivering Your Message

Delivering a concise and persuasive message is what negotiating is all about, so choose your words carefully. The other party must be able to hear what you are saying, see the value you bring, and be motivated to move toward an agreement. Listen to their feedback and watch their body language to determine if your message is being accepted and coming across in a positive way. If the other side appears to be interested in your terms but seems to be reluctant in moving forward, ask yourself if the other side may see you as aggressive. If so, restate your message with less emotion. If you still believe that you are not making headway, ask for a break. Then ask your negotiating team member(s) for feedback. *Am I coming across too strong or aggressive? Is my behavior appearing to be ego driven? How can we rephrase our message so that the other side is more receptive?* This feedback is valuable in moving forward with the negotiation. If you are coming across as too strong or ego-driven, Chapter 3 will assist you in understanding how to deal with emotional traps, your own ego, and ego-driven people. Emotions play a key role in negotiations and are notorious for throwing major curve balls in the negotiation. Having non-aggressive behavior creates a cooperative environment and makes the negotiation process more productive. Negative and aggressive emotions will only prolong the negotiation and potentially sabotage the deal.

Preparing for Your Negotiations

Always take the appropriate time to prepare for your negotiation. Prior to each meeting, make sure your team knows the information that will be discussed and disclosed, each of their roles, who will be the one negotiating, and who will be allowed to provide information in the negotiation. Never assume your team members know the information that is not to be disclosed. By making an *assumption* that your team members are well informed, you could potentially provide wrong information or disclose critical information that could change or hinder the terms of the deal. This is one assumption that could cost you severely. By being well prepared, you will have the confidence and knowledge to influence the direction of the negotiation.

It is important to review and evaluate your strategy before and after each negotiation. After each negotiation, determine whether your strategy has changed direction. Update your strategy and ingredients accordingly. Remember, if you are working on a complex deal, it is essential that the information you gathered is well organized so that you can maintain accurate records. By documenting the information obtained at each meeting, you will have the upper hand in negotiating. Organized documentation makes it possible to understand the true value of the deal, all the issues surrounding the deal, and the items agreed upon between parties. By perfecting your strategy, taking notes and keeping track of what went well and what did not, you enable yourself to orchestrate the

The Recipe: The Negotiation Strategy

negotiation. You are just like a chef perfecting her recipe. By taking notes and keeping track of what added value to the taste and what did not, she is then able to create a better soup the next time.

Chapter 3

Critical Success Factors

A skilled negotiator knows how to play the negotiating game by maneuvering through the other side's tactics and creating an agreement that is beneficial to both parties. Some negotiations are very simple and require little effort, while others are more complex and require a bit of finesse to close. This chapter provides some critical factors to consider during the negotiation process. These factors include **the power of emotions, emotional intelligence, managing the ego, overcoming fear, and patience.** Understanding these critical success factors will have a positive influence in your negotiating abilities.

The Power of Emotions

Emotions are a powerful tool in negotiation and in the cooking world because emotions influence behaviors which can cause a variety of outcomes. Enthusiasm and positive emotions encourage people to work together, while negative and aggressive emotions discourage people from working collaboratively. By creating positive emotions, you encourage the other side to feel excited about creating a mutually desirable agreement or tasting a delicious bowl of chicken soup.

Strong emotion produces strong energy and the people around you will feel your emotional energy. When you are emotionally charged about someone or something, pay attention to the amount of energy you are projecting and how the people around you react. Is your emotional energy causing your behavior to produce positive expectations, hopefulness, optimism, passion, doubt, blame, anger, hatred, jealousy, or insecurity? By being conscious of how your emotions engender certain behaviors, you can then start to monitor the amount of emotional energy you project and recognize how it affects the people around you. Understanding your emotional energy enables you to manage the outcomes of situations maturely. Always try to create a cooperative environment to negotiate. Negotiations are often stressful, even in an amicable environment, so why make it more stressful by creating and maintaining a rigid or aggressive environment.

Negative emotional energy can cause the other side to feel angry, doubtful, defensive, or insecure. Producing these types of reactions in others will only impede the negotiation from moving forward or interfere with the creativity of cooking a magnificent meal. An awareness of your emotions and the energy your emotions generate makes it possible to change negative outcomes in negotiation. When the negotiation becomes negative or unpleasant, changing the intensity of your emotional energy can assist you in turning the negotiation around. For example, if the person on the other side is emotional, with an uncontrollable temper, the best way to defuse those negative and aggressive emotions is to remain calm and not allow his behavior to trigger your emotions, which can be very difficult to do. One way to block negative energy is to keep your energy neutral or positive. Stay in a positive frame of mind while listening and acknowledging the other person's perspective. You do not have to agree with him, but by validating what he says, you help him to start relaxing his emotions (Dr. Dyer, pg. 106). If he is still adamant about remaining emotionally aggressive and negative, ask that the meeting be rescheduled and set a new date immediately. Negative energy will drain you emotionally and physically which is not good for your health or a successful negotiation.

When you become emotionally charged during a negotiation, take an immediate break for at least 15 to 30 minutes. If you take a break, the energy in the room will often change. During the break, you have a choice: stay emotionally charged, which will produce more negative energy, or focus on relaxing yourself. To relax yourself, take deep breaths, think pleasant thoughts, or go for a 5 to 10 minute walk if you can. Remember you are the only person who can allow someone or something to upset you—the choice is yours. Once you are somewhat calm, re-enter the negotiation room. Negative energy can only survive or increase if more negative energy is produced. By changing your emotional energy to a state of calmness and moving the conversation in a positive direction, you can transform the negative energy into a spirit of cooperation.

In the negotiating room, the energy generated by emotions will have a major influence on both parties' receptiveness toward moving forward with an agreeable deal. Negative or aggressive energy will cause both sides to be defensive and could easily block opportunities in seeking agreeable solutions. When it comes to finding workable solutions, positive energy opens the flood gates for the flow of creativity and new ideas to spill over and flourish.

Paying attention to your emotional energy and observing how it improves or deteriorates your situation requires patience and dedication. Learning how to change your emotional energy to a relaxed state takes a great deal of practice and determination. When observing your emotional energy, you will have the opportunity to identify and understand what triggers you emotionally. Emotional triggers often stem from historical wounds which you may or may not want to deal with. Within time, working on emotional wounds will make you less susceptible and more in control of your emotions. Additionally, you will have a better understanding of how to deal with the other side's emotions because of what you have learned about yourself. Learning about the power of your emotions is an opportunity for inner growth. In negotiation, managing your emotions in a mature manner and understanding the role emotions play are critical.

Emotional Intelligence

Emotional intelligence is a key component in negotiating successfully and being an empowering and flexible leader. In her kitchen, a chef's emotional demeanor personalizes the environment. A negotiator's emotional demeanor personalizes the negotiation process. The chef's emotional maturity plays a critical part in creating a work environment that is open-minded, friendly, and relaxing. This type of atmosphere engenders teamwork, creativity, and flexibility and produces innovative chicken soups.

Displaying emotional intelligence in negotiations can be very effective and powerful, since negotiations tend to trigger emotions that bring out the best or worst behaviors people are capable of exhibiting. Emotional intelligence involves managing your emotions and behavior in a mature manner, especially when dealing with difficult people or situations. On the other hand, by allowing your emotions to control your behavior, your behavior could become destructive and potentially cause you to lose the deal. Understanding the power of emotions and the effect they have in the negotiation process gives you an advantage in negotiating with difficult people or situations. An awareness of the impact that emotions can display along with the consequences allows you to skillfully maneuver through emotionally charged situations. The reality is that our thoughts persuade our emotions, which, in turn, drive our actions. When negotiating, you should always be cognitive of how your emotions are being perceived by the other side so that you can gauge them and your behavior. This awareness will assist you in steering a negotiation in a positive direction.

Attitude

When negotiating, your attitude plays a major role in how it affects your emotions which, in turn, affects whether you have a positive or negative approach. In other words, your attitude can influence how your emotions play out. If you are well rested, alert, and happy, you will have a better disposition and an open mind. You can handle issues or unpleasant news in a more calm and mature manner. If you are tired, hungry, upset, or angry, try to postpone the negotiation. You do not want your emotions to be easily triggered in a negative way and cause the negotiation to move in the wrong direction. Take the time to think about your attitude and disposition before entering into any negotiation room.

If you are hungry, eat something before entering the negotiation. You do not want your mind on food instead of the information that is being exchanged in the negotiation. You need to be alert in order to protect yourself or your company from unfavorable terms and conditions that arise. Additionally, being hungry will heighten your emotions and could cause you to react in an unpleasant manner. Negotiations require energy and can easily drain you emotionally, so get enough rest and food before you negotiate.

If you are upset or angry, either change your disposition or postpone the meeting. Managing your emotions when you are already upset or angry is extremely difficult. You run the risk of saying or doing something that could hinder the deal. Take time to think about your emotional state and determine whether you can control your emotions. It is better to be safe than sorry. Once the damage is done, it may be impossible to undo.

Managing Conflicts

Usually negotiations never go according to plan because something usually happens to change the itinerary or direction of the negotiation. Changes entice conflicts and are an integral part of the negotiation. Conflicts are productive if handled in a mature manner. Conflicts allow both parties to debate issues, concessions, and constraints. The debating process, along with being open minded, engenders resolution. When conflicts occur and are not handled in a mature manner, it is usually because people tend to take things personally as well as wanting to be right. Well, negotiation is not about being right. As mentioned earlier, your goal in negotiation is to create a profitable deal in which the other side is satisfied with the agreement—*not* to win arguments. If you become emotional during this time, remember this is just a business deal and adhere to the facts. Your goal is to stay focused and manage your emotions so that you can be receptive to solutions that could resolve the conflict hampering the deal. Do not allow your emotions or ego to obstruct the negotiation. Try to make a conscious decision about how to react so that you always behave in an emotionally mature manner.

Managing the Ego

We all have egos. Some people display theirs more than others. The ego plays a major role in most of our lives but can be detrimental to our negotiations and to the work environment of the chef's kitchen. People with strong, dominating egos generate emotional energy that often feels unpleasant to others. A strong and aggressive ego works to achieve goals, usually at any cost and is not open to all possibilities or opportunities. When you are ego driven in a negotiation, you are headed towards trouble! You become unbendable and unreasonable, producing a rigid environment to negotiate in and turning people away from your ideas or solutions. Negotiation can only move forward if both parties are willing to work together to find an agreeable solution. Do not allow yours or the other side's ego to impede the deal from moving forward. Use your emotional intelligence to understand the other side's ego. In *Change Your Thoughts, Change Your Life*, Dr. Wayne Dyer (pg. 106) explains how to dismiss the ego's attitude and create a trusting atmosphere:

> When you live from the perspective of being able to say, "I don't know for certain, but I'm willing to listen," you become a person whom others identify with. Why? Because your flexibility lets them see that their point of view is welcome. By being open to all possibilities, everyone who encounters you feels their ideas are valuable and there's no need for conflict.

The trust and respect of both parties who manage their egos allow the negotiation to move forward into an open atmosphere where creativity flows. Always listen to your intuition (gut instincts) for guidance and *not* your ego.

If the other side is playing manipulative, emotional games in order to throw you off track to control you and the negotiation, try not to let their controlling behavior irritate or affect you. Remind yourself that this is game and no one can control you unless you allow them. At times, we forget this and get upset. First, examine the situation and ask yourself if you agree with what the other side is saying or doing. If you agree, then recognize that you made the decision to agree, so you are not being controlled. If you disagree, then make sure to state your position to avoid being controlled and do not allow yourself to get upset. By working through this exercise, you empower yourself to make conscious decisions about how you should react. Your conscious decisions will influence the consequences of your reactions, usually in a positive manner. Another tactic is to find ways to let the other side think they are in control of the negotiation. Perceptions are not always correct. Control is all about the ego. The ego makes you feel superior over others, giving the illusion that you need to control the situation (Dyer, pg. 141). No one likes to feel he is being controlled. When either party allows his ego to control the negotiation, working toward an agreement becomes extremely hard (if not impossible). By managing your emotions, you are able to stay focused allowing you to direct the negotiation constructively.

Observing your ego behavior is not a pleasant task. Here is a question to ask yourself. "Do you like working with someone who is egotistical?" If the answer is "no," then take time to observe whether your ego is controlling your behavior, particularly if you notice that the other side is not receptive to your ideas or solutions. The ego makes you feel important and powerful, but remember it is simply an illusion. Do not get caught up in believing you have control of the deal when your ego is enforced as such behavior can disappoint you in the end. Things may appear to be working out for a time, but eventually your ego will have a negative effect on the negotiation. When you truly trust your intuition to guide you, deals will work to your advantage.

Trusting your intuition is not an easy task and it takes time and patience to develop your intuitional skills. This does not happen overnight. However, it is important to distinguish your intuition from your ego. Recognize that your ego is completely selfish and greedy. Intuition guides you to read the environment and make decisions based on your internal heartfelt reactions to that environment. Listening to your intuition for guidance can be scary at times, especially if you do not have a clear direction on how to move forward. Have patience with yourself to allow enough time for your intuition to guide you. As you learn to recognize and trust your intuition, you will possess the inner strength and confidence to create lucrative deals or to walk away from unprofitable deals. People will enjoy making deals with you because there is a peacefulness that radiates from you and allows them to trust you.

Understanding emotions and trusting your intuition will assist you in reading people, predicting the outcomes of situations, and knowing if you can trust them. Having the ability to read people and predict outcomes will give you an advantage in negotiating and in flavoring your soup to accommodate your customer's taste.

Overcoming Fear

Fear may be the number one factor that causes people to give in too quickly in a negotiation and causes chefs to be ultra conservative with the meals they prepare. Fear makes you become doubtful of your ability to negotiate a situation or to try new techniques and flavors in cooking. You begin second guessing your strategy and becoming anxious under the pressure of trying to close the deal. If you investigate and document all your negotiating ingredients upfront along with an alternative plan, you will have greater confidence to negotiate and communicate effectively regarding any issues that arise. You will know how to proceed in the negotiation process and be better equipped to handle surprises as they appear. When you are unprepared, fear sets in because of all the unknowns. Having the appropriate knowledge is powerful and can reduce your fears, so take the time to prepare for your negotiation. For a chef, the organization, preparation, and planning of a meal are the key elements in having confidence in cooking delicious meals on a consistent basis.

Fear is just an illusion. How you perceive yourself and your situation will dictate if fear is present within you. The next time you become afraid ask, "What is the worst thing that could happen in this situation?" or "Why am I so afraid?" By asking yourself these questions, you start understanding where your fears are coming from and testing their realism. Having alternative options can assist you in diminishing some of your fears. You may consider talking to people you can trust to work through your concerns or fears. Make the decision to understand and manage your fears rather than allowing your fears to control you.

Patience

Patience is a virtue when it comes to cooking a fabulous pot of chicken soup because it takes preparation and adequate time (up to 4 hours) to cook (Chef Robyne). A skilled negotiator will possess patience and flexibility just like a chef. Chef Robyne states that her mother always said, "a watched pot never boils." This statement is also applicable to negotiating. Constantly monitoring your negotiation deadline will not make the process go any faster. Negotiations have a tendency to take longer than anticipated and will test your level of patience. When the negotiation keeps getting prolonged, ask direct questions such as, "What are your key issues or concerns that need to be resolved in order to come to an agreement?" The answer you receive from the other side will let you know if you are headed in the right direction and will give you a better idea of how much longer the negotiation could proceed.

Trying to control the negotiation timeframe can be very stressful. If you are on a rigid timeframe, you will benefit when you consider time as a non-negotiable item. If time is not a deal breaker, then having patience will work to your advantage because you will not give away value or pay too much in order to capture the deal quickly. People with little patience have a tendency to either discount or over-pay in order to secure the deal within *their* timeframe. Next time you negotiate, observe your behavior to determine how much patience you have, and to see if you are making hasty decisions that cause you to give away or pay too much. You just may learn some valuable information about your patience level and how it influences your negotiation abilities.

Chapter 4

Closing the Deal

Closing the deal may not always be the final piece of the negotiation. Sometimes negotiation continues after closing. This is common among certain cultures or for complex deals in which the details of the deal are finalized after closing the deal. By now, the hard-work you have put into investigating your ingredients and developing a powerful strategy have made it possible for you to have the confidence in negotiating effectively. Arguably, closing the deal begins when both parties present their terms and conditions. This occurs when negotiating becomes challenging and often frustrating, but many believe that closing is the most exciting part of the negotiation. You will enjoy this part if you think of negotiating as a business game and do not get emotionally involved. During this time, people have a tendency to get nervous, feel insecure, doubt their negotiating ability, or allow their ego to control the situation. A person who enjoys building relationships during negotiations and avoids conflicts at all costs, often backing down when confronted with challenging issues, may not enjoy this aspect of the negotiation. Closing deals is not for everyone, but you can still add value to the negotiation by assisting in the investigation and documentation, in developing the strategy, by providing critical feedback, and many other important functions.

When trying to close a deal, you must constantly still seek knowledge about the other side's interests and motives along with unforeseen events that could delay or damage the deal. Keep in mind that closing deals can be a very long and tedious process. Always pay close attention as new information is unfolded to ensure that modification to your strategy is not required and that you account for all financial and liability risks. The closing phase is the time to extract the most value from your concessions. Remember to first trade the items that have the lowest value to you. Understanding the value you trade from your concession list will play a crucial role in how you determine and structure your terms and conditions.

Finalizing an Agreement

Knowing when to finalize an agreement is similar to knowing when the chicken soup texture, flavor, and seasoning are in harmony, which means the soup is ready to be served. (Chef Robyne) In negotiating, always trust your intuition, watch for clues, and listen to the types of questions the other side asks. Are they asking about delivery time, resource availability, payment terms, or a starting date? These types of questions indicate that they are preparing themselves mentally to close on the deal. Once both parties resolve issues to a point of agreement, the deal is then ready to be finalized.

When wrapping up the deal, create a summary of commercial and contractual terms and conditions to present to the other side for their approval. Once both parties agree to the terms and conditions, offer to draft the contract or agreement so that you control the language of the document. In addition to maintaining control of how the agreement is written, you make it more difficult for the other side to hide unacceptable terms and conditions.

Lessons Learned

Once a negotiation process has been completed, whether or not a deal has been made, take the time to do a lesson learned. This exercise is extremely valuable in understanding your strengths and weaknesses. Keep it simple by listing what worked well in the negotiation and what areas require improvements. Making an assessment of your negotiation strengths and weaknesses is one of the fastest ways to improve your negotiation skills and maintain proficiency in extracting the most value on a consistent basis.

The best way to prevent mistakes from repeating is to develop a "Contract Pitfalls" list which provides your industry's unfavorable commercial and contractual terms and conditions. The "Contract Pitfalls" list should be reviewed during the negotiation and updated after each negotiation, if applicable. By having a list of contract pitfalls, you will save tremendous amounts of time and money in the future. The "Contract Pitfall" list is just another way of protecting yourself from unacceptable terms that could cost you or your company unnecessary time and money.

Chapter 5

Negotiating with Different Cultures

As previously mentioned, the various types of pots used to cook the chicken soup represent negotiating with different cultures. Just as when a chef uses a different type of pot to cook her chicken soup, she has to alter the way the soup is cooked. When you negotiate with another culture, you may need to alter the way you negotiate. The material of a pot is paramount when it comes to determining the temperature and the amount of time to cook the soup (Chef Robyne). A chef must be knowledgeable about the material of the pot she chooses in order not to risk burning her delicious pot of chicken soup.

Negotiating with different cultures may create more complexity and challenges to overcome, but can be extremely exciting and educational. Knowledge about the other side's business and cultural etiquette and regimes is mandatory in order for you to negotiate effectively and come to an agreeable contract or agreement. Understanding a country's culture and mannerisms is just as important as understanding the company with whom you are negotiating. Before negotiating with a company of a different culture, investigate and learn what types of things may be *different* from what you are accustomed to dealing with. They may include:

General Mannerisms
- Proper greetings
- Dining decorum
- Rituals
- Taboos
- Values

Business Mannerisms
- Proper greetings
- Meeting etiquette
- Proper correspondence
- Negotiating decorum, strategies, and tactics
- Motivating factors

Country Regimes
- Government
- Politics
- Economics
- Stability

Learning this information will enhance your negotiation position and provide an understanding of how the negotiation game is played among different cultures and countries. This information can be obtained through the World-Wide Web (www), international organizations in your industries, colleagues that have dealt with international clients, the News, business and culture magazines, newspapers within the country where you seek to conduct business, and books on different cultures. The book *When Cultures Collide* by Richard D. Lewis provides a wealth of information about some of the topics stated above for over 80 countries. Another good book is *Kiss, Bow, or Shake Hands: ASIA* by Terri Morrison and Wayne A. Conaway.

When negotiating with another culture, you still have to investigate and document all your ingredients: non-negotiable items, assumptions, constraints, concessions, negotiating abilities, and competitors. More time will be required to address assumptions and constraints. You must determine the potential risks in regard to legal, political, financial, environmental, and security concerns or issues. More information about these risks is provided later in this chapter.

General and Business Mannerisms

Think back to the blending section of the negotiation recipe. If you recall, the water portion of the chicken soup represents trust, integrity, and respect in the negotiation. The seasoning represents the negotiating abilities which are emotional intelligence, positive attitude, enthusiasm, good communication and listening skills and many more. Negotiating in different cultures relies on these aspects of negotiation.

Respect and integrity have different meanings in different cultures. If you ignore or fail to understand the importance of the cultural mannerisms, you could easily insult or behave disrespectfully to the other side and not even be aware of it. Behaving disrespectfully in a person's culture could have a negative impact on the negotiation process and could potentially end the negotiation. Spend time understanding what respect and integrity mean in the country in which you wish to conduct business. There are hundreds of examples to show how effortless it can be to do something disrespectful in another culture and be clueless about it. Here are two very simple examples that demonstrate how easily you could act disrespectfully in another culture before the negotiation even begins:

Example 1:

In certain countries when a person provides you with a business card, you should accept the card in following manner, because any other action could be considered disrespectful:

- Look at the card, then immediately read the information.
- Look the person directly in the eye to confirm that you have acknowledged the information and his/her position.

(If you take the person's business card and immediately place it in your pocket or briefcase without acknowledging the information on the card, this person will consider your behavior disrespectful and may choose not to do business with you.)

Example 2:

In some cultures if you sit with your legs crossed and show the bottom of your shoe, you are showing disrespect to the person with whom you are speaking.

These are two simple examples of how to begin a negotiation with the wrong impression. By showing disrespect, you could easily trigger the other side emotionally, causing unforeseen problems. How a culture handles emotions may be completely different from how you handle them. Not being aware of the mannerisms of the country you are conducting business in can make your negotiation extremely difficult or even impossible. Making assumptions that other countries conduct business similar to yours will get you into trouble and possibly negate the deal. Therefore, spend adequate time learning as much as possible about the other side's general and business mannerisms and be open to changing your behavior to show respect for the other person's culture.

Every country employs different negotiation strategies and tactics. These strategies and tactics are influenced by negotiating abilities. Your negotiating skills may be tested at a completely new level. If you prefer to be in the driver's seat of the negotiation, then educating yourself about the other side's negotiating abilities, motivating factors, negotiating decorum, strategies, and tactics is highly necessary. A person who has a macro view of the deal, along with the critical variables, has the upper hand in the negotiation. Such a person has a clear understanding of the terms and conditions of the deal and recognizes how to construct a strategy to extract the most value from the deal. If you are unaware of the other side's negotiation tactics and motivating factors, then extracting value from the deal may be more challenging than you anticipate.

Country Regimes

The stability of a country's political environment, government, and financials are crucial when determining the profitability of a deal. Plenty of deals abroad can be attractive at the beginning, but contractual, political, and financial implications can cause the deal to become economically unfeasible. When conducting your economic scenarios, make sure you cover all your exposed risk. Be aware that tax laws and regulations can easily be changed in any country, so make sure the economic scenarios reflect different types of tax implications and financial liabilities if required, or include protection clauses in your agreement. Here is an example of items used to identify risks that may impact a deal's economics:

- Government and Local Taxes
- Government Laws and Regulations
- Natural Resources Taxes
- Percentage of Royalty Paid to the other Company and Government
- Import and Export Taxes
- Security Cost (Strikes, kidnapping, riots, acts of war, etc.)
- Financial Liabilities due to Legal or Contractual Issues
- Environmental Laws
- Delay of Payment
- Exchange Control, Convertibility of Currency

Make sure you investigate all your potential risks since the economics are the most important aspect of the deal. If there is no money to be made, it is best to know up-front before you invest too much of your time and money. This is one area to ensure that your economist or financial expert accounts for all potential risks and liabilities of the deal. Once the results of the economic scenarios are presented, then the appropriate decision can be made as to how to proceed in the negotiation—whether to move forward with or terminate the deal.

Conducting business deals in a foreign country can be very perplexing and challenging. Depending upon the complexity of your deal, obtaining legal, financial, political, environmental, and security expertise about the country in which you wish to conduct business will assist you in identifying all your potential risks. Negotiating is about having fun while extracting the best value for you. Investigate your ingredients, know whom you are negotiating with along with the culture mannerisms, and develop a powerful strategy that will assist you in formulating a mutually agreed upon contract.

Chapter 6

Negotiating Tips

This chapter provides a summary of negotiating tips from the previous chapters. The same summary of negotiating tips is reprised in the back of the book so that you can remove the sheets and take with you, if needed.

Recipe for Negotiating Business Deals Successfully

RECIPE

For Negotiating a Business Deal (Chicken Soup)

Ingredients:

- Non-negotiables
- Constraints 
- Assumptions 
- Concession List 
- Competitors <Influencers> 
- Negotiating Ability 

Analyze: Yours and the Other Side's Ingredients

Mix:

Add:  Alternative Plan

Blend: Integrity, Trust, Respect

with: Enthusiasm, Emotional Intelligence, Positive Attitude, Good Communication & Listening Skills, Good Record Keeping (Seasoning)

Negotiate (Cook): Extract the Most Value (Create a Delicious Soup)

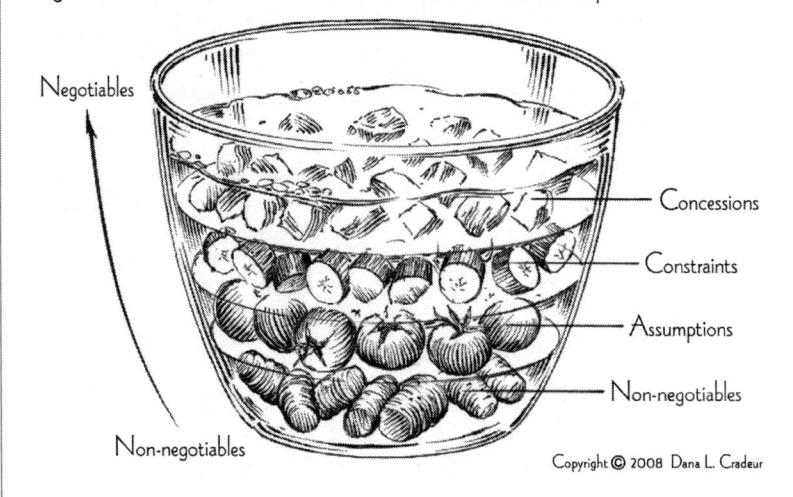

- Negotiables
- Concessions
- Constraints
- Assumptions
- Non-negotiables
- Non-negotiables

Copyright © 2008 Dana L. Cradeur

Recipe for Negotiating a Business Deal *(Chicken Soup)*

Ingredients
Non-negotiables *(Carrots)*, Assumptions *(Tomatoes)*,
Constraints *(Zucchini)*, Concession List *(Chicken)*,
Competitors *(Onions)*, Negotiating Ability *(Seasoning)*

Analyze
Yours and The Other Side's Ingredients

Mix
(Carrots, Tomatoes, Zucchinis, Chicken, Onions)

Add
Alternative Plan *(Beef)*

Blend
Integrity, Trust, Respect *(Water)*

with

Enthusiasm, Emotional Intelligence, Positive Attitude,
Good Communication and Listening Skills,
Patience *(Seasoning)*

Negotiate *(Cook)*
Extracting the Most Value *(Creating a Delicious Taste)*

Recipe for Negotiating Business Deals Successfully

Non-Negotiable Items
- Non-negotiable items are any commercial or contractual terms and conditions that must be adhered to in order to proceed with the deal.
- Both parties' non-negotiable items should be defined and presented at the beginning of the negotiation so that little time and money are wasted.

Assumptions
- An Assumption is something that you believe could be true about the other side or a situation.
- Assumptions are not facts until proven, so test all your assumptions.

Constraints
- A constraint is a potential risk and/or liability with financial and/or contractual implications if not resolved or mitigated properly.
- Exposed risks could cost you in the millions if not identified and resolved or mitigated during the negotiation.

Concessions
- A concession is any item, service, or location that is considered negotiable. Examples: Price, Quality, Costs, Time, Services, Location, etc.
- Everything is negotiable except your non-negotiable items.
- Vendor and buyer concession lists help you to stay focused on the values you can extract from the deal.
- The negotiation scorecard informs you of how lucrative the deal was for you and how much money was left on the table or given away.

Negotiating Abilities
- Negotiating abilities are comprised of emotional intelligence, enthusiasm, quick thinking, team player, investigating, strategizing, creativity, good record keeping, good listening and communication skills.
- Creating a positive and friendly atmosphere allows people to relax and communication has a tendency to be more open and trusting.
- Always be cognizant of how your behavior is being perceived by the other side.
- Understanding the other side's negotiating abilities is a key ingredient in developing your negotiation strategy and tactics.

Competitors
- Understanding the overall picture of what your competitors are doing and the tactics used against you in negotiating is extremely important in determining how you should structure the deal.

By documenting, updating, and modifying all the ingredients stated above, you stay ahead of the game and become more confident in your decisions regarding how to steer the direction of the negotiation.

Alternative Plan
- An alternative plan provides you another option if an agreement cannot be met.
- Without an alternative plan, people have a tendency to feel more pressure to secure a deal whether the deal is profitable or not especially if the deal is worth a large sum of money.
- Always try to discover what the other side's alternative plan is.

Integrity, Respect, and Trust
- Integrity, Respect, and Trust are essential virtues when negotiating business deals in any culture.
- Integrity and respect have different meanings in different cultures.

Negotiation Strategy
Questions to assist you in developing your strategy:
- What are the key steps to accomplishing your goal?
- What is the true value of the deal?
- What are your top 3 - 5 concessions you will consider trading if required?
- What are your top 3 - 5 concessions you prefer not to trade?
- What are the terms and conditions you plan to offer?
- What is your timeframe in closing the deal?
- What is the other side's timeframe in closing the deal?
- How will you structure the deal?
- How will you present your offer?
- What message do you wish to deliver?
- How do you think the other side will react to your offer?
- Who is on your negotiation team?
- Who is the lead negotiator?

As new information unfolds, evaluate your strategy to determine if any modifications are required.

The Power of Emotions
- Negotiations have a way of bringing out the best and worst behavior in people, because emotions have a tendency to be triggered easily.
- Allowing your emotions to control your behavior may be destructive and could potentially cause you to lose the deal.
- Negative emotions projected could cause the other side to feel angry, doubtful, defensive, or insecure which will hinder the negotiation from moving forward.

- The best way to defuse negative and aggressive emotions is to remain calm and take a 15 to 30 minute break from negotiating. Take deep breaths, think pleasant thoughts and/or take a brief walk.
- Negative energy can only survive or increase if more negative emotions are produced.
- Negative energy will drain you emotionally and physically which is not good for your health or a successful negotiation.

Emotional Intelligence
- Emotional intelligence is managing your emotions and behavior in a mature manner, especially when dealing with difficult people or situations.
- By being well rested, alert, and happy, you will have a better disposition and an open mind in handling issues or unpleasant news.
- If you are angry or upset, try to postpone the negotiation to another time or day until you have had enough time to calm yourself, because your emotions are already heightened and could easily impede the deal.
- Negotiations require energy, so make sure you get enough rest and food before you negotiate.

The Ego
- People with strong, dominating egos generate emotional energy that often feels unpleasant to others.
- Egos cause people to be unbendable and unreasonable which produces a rigid environment to negotiate in and turns people away from your ideas or solutions.
- Always be aware of your ego in order to determine if your ego is controlling your behavior particularly if the other side is not receptive to your ideas or solutions.
- Your intuition is your inner compass so always follow it and not your ego.

Overcoming Fear
- Fear is all about the unknown, so seek the proper knowledge to uncover the unknown.
- When you become afraid, ask, "What is the worst thing that could happen in this situation?" or "Why am I so afraid?" This helps you to understand where your fears are coming from. If you come up with solutions or alternative options, your fear will start to subside.

Conflicts
- Conflicts are good if handled in a mature manner.
- Conflicts allow both parties to debate issues, constraints, and concessions.

Delivering Your Message
- The other party must be able to hear what you are saying, see the value you bring, and be motivated to move toward an agreement.
- If your message is not being accepted, ask yourself, "Are my emotions too strong or aggressive? Is my behavior ego driven?"

Finalizing the Contract
- Create a summary of the commercial and contractual terms and conditions for your team and the other side to review and approve.
- Offer to draft the contract or agreement, so you can control the language and the other side cannot easily hide unacceptable terms.
- Review your "Contract Pitfalls" list to ensure you are not repeating any past contractual and commercial mistakes.

Negotiating Tips

Negotiating with Different Cultures

Thoroughly investigate and understand the following culture mannerisms and regimes before negotiating:

General Mannerisms
- Proper greetings
- Dining decorum
- Rituals
- Taboos
- Values

Business Mannerisms
- Proper greetings
- Meeting etiquette
- Proper correspondences
- Negotiating decorum, strategies, and tactics
- Motivating factors

Country Regimes
- Political Stability
- Government and Local Taxes
- Government Laws and Regulations
- Natural Resources Taxes
- Percentage of Royalty Paid to the other Company and Government
- Import and Export Taxes
- Security Cost (Strikes, kidnapping, riots, acts of wars, and etc.)
- Financial Liabilities due to Legal or Contractual Issues
- Environmental Laws
- Delay of Payment
- Exchange Control, Convertibility of Currency

References

Trump Style Negotiation: Powerful Strategies and Tactics for Mastering Every Deal, George H. Ross, (Copyright © George H. Ross) p. 148, 36, 133, 20, and 3. "Reprinted with permission of John Wiley & Sons, Inc."

Change Your Thoughts — Change Your Life, Dr. Wayne W. Dyer, (Copyright © 2007) p. 106 and 141. Carlsbad, CA: Hayhouse, Inc.

Author's interview with Chef Robyne Befeld in Jackson Hole, WY, 2008.

Author's interview with Banquet Chef John Wentworth at Spring Creek Ranch in Jackson Hole, WY, 2008.

Appendix

Worksheet 1

Non-Negotiables (Carrots)	
Your Non-Negotiables	Other Side's Non-Negotiables

Assumptions (Tomatoes)		
Assumptions	Tested (Yes/No)	Date Confirmed

Constraints (Zucchini)				
Constraints	Risk (High/Med/Low)	Mitigation Plan	Other Side's Constraints	Risk (High/Med/Low)

Worksheet II

Vendor							
Concession List (Chicken)				Terms and Conditions			
Priority	Standard Concession	Concessions to Trade	Value to the Other Side (High, Med, Low $)	Value to You (High, Med, Low $)	T&C to Present to the Other Side	Goal	Unacceptable T&C or Deal Breaker

Buyer						
Concession List (Chicken)				Terms and Conditions		
Priority	Concessions to Trade	Value to the Other Side (High, Med, Low $)	Value to You (High, Med, Low $)	T&C to Present to the Other Side	Goal	Unacceptable T&C or Deal Breaker

Negotiation Scorecard				
Item No.	What Have You Actually Traded or Given Away?	$ Value Given to the Other Side (Revenue Loss)	What Has the Other Side Given to You?	Value to You in $ (High, Medium, Low)

Worksheet III

Other Side Negotiating Ability (Seasoning)									
Names	Emotions Displayed (Calm, Pleasant, Aggressive, Angry, Others)	Tactics Used in Negotiating	Trustworthy (Yes/No)	Decision Maker (Yes/No)	Track Record (Good, Avg, Poor, Unknown)	Subject Matter Expert (Yes/Somewhat/No/Unknown)	Decision Required Soon (Yes/No)	Complaints

Competitor (Onions)				
Competitor	Price	Deal Constraints	Motives	Concessions They are Willing to Give Away or Trade

Recipe for Negotiating Business Deals Successfully

Dear Negotiator,

I hope you enjoyed reading this book as much as I enjoyed writing it and being able to meet some wonderful chefs. My goal was to write a book that is simple, easy-to-use, and portable for traveling, since negotiating has so many intricate facets and the amount of information obtained can be easy to forget and cumbersome at times. By comparing negotiating with cooking chicken soup, I hope you are now able to remember most of the ingredients required to negotiate successfully. Also remember to be flexible and open minded, manage your emotions and ego, and most of all to have fun.

I wish you all the very best in your future negotiations.

Dana L. Cradeur

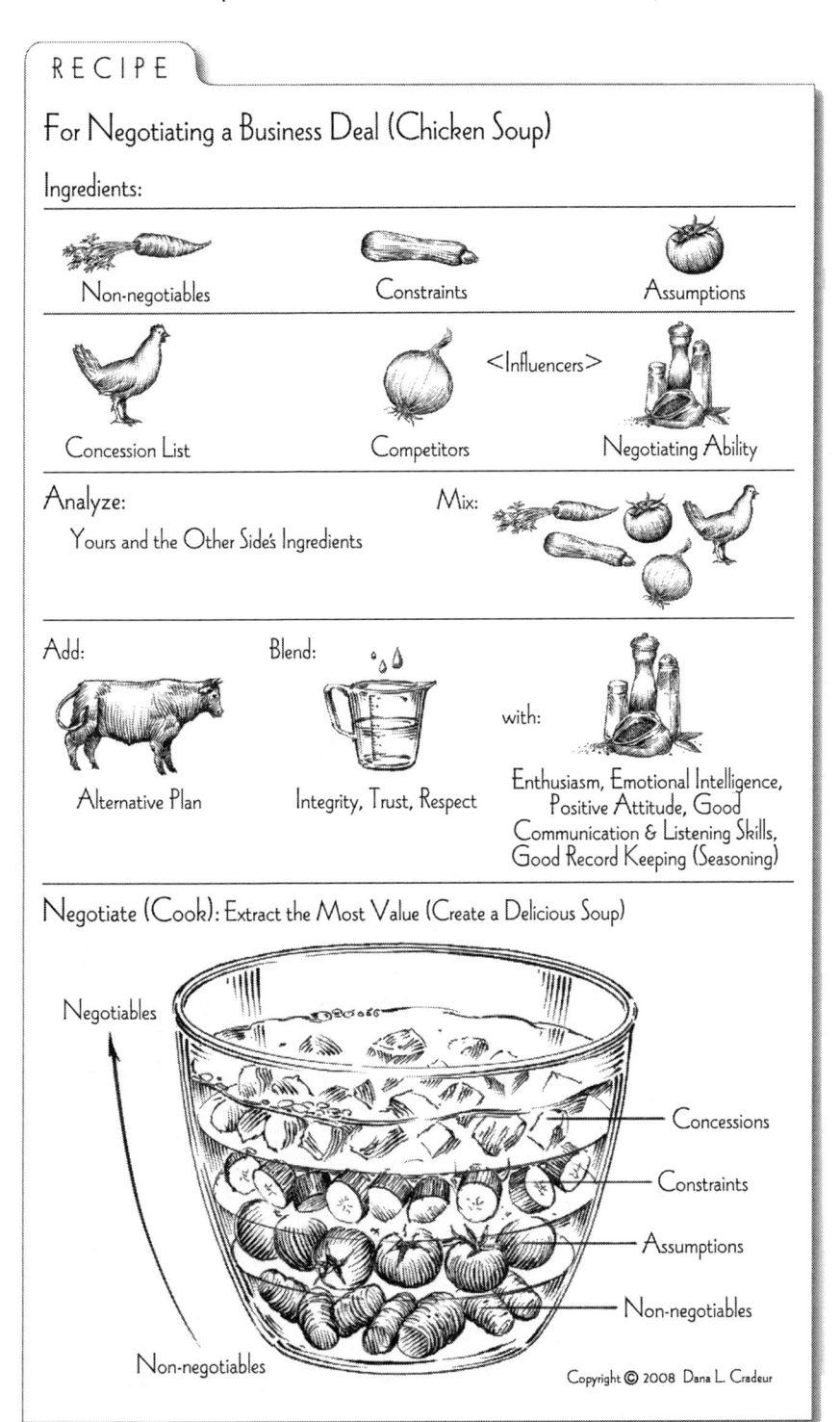

Recipe for Negotiating Business Deals Successfully

RECIPE

For Negotiating a Business Deal (Chicken Soup)

Ingredients:

- Non-negotiables
- Constraints
- Assumptions
- Concession List
- Competitors <Influencers>
- Negotiating Ability

Analyze: Yours and the Other Side's Ingredients

Mix:

Add: Alternative Plan

Blend: Integrity, Trust, Respect

with: Enthusiasm, Emotional Intelligence, Positive Attitude, Good Communication & Listening Skills, Good Record Keeping (Seasoning)

Negotiate (Cook): Extract the Most Value (Create a Delicious Soup)

Negotiables ↑
- Concessions
- Constraints
- Assumptions
- Non-negotiables

Non-negotiables

Copyright © 2008 Dana L. Cradeur

Copyright © 2008 Dana L. Cradeur
www.Danaiconsulting.com

Recipe for Negotiating Business Deals Successfully

Recipe for Negotiating a Business Deal (Chicken Soup)

Ingredients
Non-negotiables *(Carrots)*, Assumptions *(Tomatoes)*,
Constraints *(Zucchini)*, Concession List *(Chicken)*,
Competitors *(Onions)*, Negotiating Ability *(Seasoning)*

Analyze
Yours and The Other Side's Ingredients

Mix
(Carrots, Tomatoes, Zucchinis, Chicken, Onions)

Add
Alternative Plan *(Beef)*

Blend
Integrity, Trust, Respect *(Water)*
with
Enthusiasm, Emotional Intelligence, Positive Attitude,
Good Communication and Listening Skills,
Patience *(Seasoning)*

Negotiate (Cook)
Extracting the Most Value *(Creating a Delicious Taste)*

Copyright © 2008 Dana L. Cradeur
www.Danaiconsulting.com

Recipe for Negotiating Business Deals Successfully

Non-Negotiable Items
- Non-negotiable items are any commercial or contractual terms and conditions that must be adhered to in order to proceed with the deal.
- Both parties' non-negotiable items should be defined and presented at the beginning of the negotiation so that little time and money are wasted.

Assumptions
- An Assumption is something that you believe could be true about the other side or a situation.
- Assumptions are not facts until proven, so test all your assumptions.

Constraints
- A constraint is a potential risk and/or liability with financial and/or contractual implications if not resolved or mitigated properly.
- Exposed risks could cost you in the millions if not identified and resolved or mitigated during the negotiation.

Concessions
- A concession is any item, service, or location that is considered negotiable. Examples: Price, Quality, Costs, Time, Services, Location, etc.
- Everything is negotiable except your non-negotiable items.
- Vendor and buyer concession lists help you to stay focused on the values you can extract from the deal.
- The negotiation scorecard informs you of how lucrative the deal was for you and how much money was left on the table or given away.

Copyright © 2008 Dana L. Cradeur
www.Danaiconsulting.com

Recipe for Negotiating Business Deals Successfully

Negotiating Abilities
- Negotiating abilities are comprised of emotional intelligence, enthusiasm, quick thinking, team player, investigating, strategizing, creativity, good record keeping, good listening and communication skills.
- Creating a positive and friendly atmosphere allows people to relax and communication has a tendency to be more open and trusting.
- Always be cognizant of how your behavior is being perceived by the other side.
- Understanding the other side's negotiating abilities is a key ingredient in developing your negotiation strategy and tactics.

Competitors
- Understanding the overall picture of what your competitors are doing and the tactics used against you in negotiating is extremely important in determining how you should structure the deal.

By documenting, updating, and modifying all the ingredients stated above, you stay ahead of the game and become more confident in your decisions regarding how to steer the direction of the negotiation.

Alternative Plan
- An alternative plan provides you another option if an agreement cannot be met.
- Without an alternative plan, people have a tendency to feel more pressure to secure a deal whether the deal is profitable or not especially if the deal is worth a large sum of money.
- Always try to discover what the other side's alternative plan is.

Copyright © 2008 Dana L. Cradeur
www.Danaiconsulting.com

Recipe for Negotiating Business Deals Successfully

Integrity, Respect, and Trust
- Integrity, Respect, and Trust are essential virtues when negotiating business deals in any culture.
- Integrity and respect have different meanings in different cultures.

Negotiation Strategy

Questions to assist you in developing your strategy:
- What are the key steps to accomplishing your goal?
- What is the true value of the deal?
- What are your top 3 - 5 concessions you will consider trading if required?
- What are your top 3 - 5 concessions you prefer not to trade?
- What are the terms and conditions you plan to offer?
- What is your timeframe in closing the deal?
- What is the other side's timeframe in closing the deal?
- How will you structure the deal?
- How will you present your offer?
- What message do you wish to deliver?
- How do you think the other side will react to your offer?
- Who is on your negotiation team?
- Who is the lead negotiator?

As new information unfolds, evaluate your strategy to determine if any modifications are required.

The Power of Emotions
- Negotiations have a way of bringing out the best and worst behavior in people, because emotions have a tendency to be triggered easily.
- Allowing your emotions to control your behavior may be destructive and could potentially cause you to lose the deal.
- Negative emotions projected could cause the other side to feel angry, doubtful, defensive, or insecure which will hinder the negotiation from moving forward.

Copyright © 2008 Dana L. Cradeur
www.Danaiconsulting.com

Recipe for Negotiating Business Deals Successfully

- The best way to defuse negative and aggressive emotions is to remain calm and take a 15 to 30 minute break from negotiating. Take deep breaths, think pleasant thoughts and/or take a brief walk.
- Negative energy can only survive or increase if more negative emotions are produced.
- Negative energy will drain you emotionally and physically which is not good for your health or a successful negotiation.

Emotional Intelligence

- Emotional intelligence is managing your emotions and behavior in a mature manner, especially when dealing with difficult people or situations.
- By being well rested, alert, and happy, you will have a better disposition and an open mind in handling issues or unpleasant news.
- If you are angry or upset, try to postpone the negotiation to another time or day until you have had enough time to calm yourself, because your emotions are already heightened and could easily impede the deal.
- Negotiations require energy, so make sure you get enough rest and food before you negotiate.

The Ego

- People with strong, dominating egos generate emotional energy that often feels unpleasant to others.
- Egos cause people to be unbendable and unreasonable which produces a rigid environment to negotiate in and turns people away from your ideas or solutions.
- Always be aware of your ego in order to determine if your ego is controlling your behavior particularly if the other side is not receptive to your ideas or solutions.
- Your intuition is your inner compass so always follow it and not your ego.

Copyright © 2008 Dana L. Cradeur
www.Danaiconsulting.com

Recipe for Negotiating Business Deals Successfully

Overcoming Fear
- Fear is all about the unknown, so seek the proper knowledge to uncover the unknown.
- When you become afraid, ask, "What is the worst thing that could happen in this situation?" or "Why am I so afraid?" This helps you to understand where your fears are coming from. If you come up with solutions or alternative options, your fear will start to subside.

Conflicts
- Conflicts are good if handled in a mature manner.
- Conflicts allow both parties to debate issues, constraints, and concessions.

Delivering Your Message
- The other party must be able to hear what you are saying, see the value you bring, and be motivated to move toward an agreement.
- If your message is not being accepted, ask yourself, "Are my emotions too strong or aggressive? Is my behavior ego driven?"

Finalizing the Contract
- Create a summary of the commercial and contractual terms and conditions for your team and the other side to review and approve.
- Offer to draft the contract or agreement, so you can control the language and the other side cannot easily hide unacceptable terms.
- Review your "Contract Pitfalls" list to ensure you are not repeating any past contractual and commercial mistakes.

Copyright © 2008 Dana L. Cradeur
www.Danaiconsulting.com

Recipe for Negotiating Business Deals Successfully

Negotiating with Different Cultures

Thoroughly investigate and understand the following culture mannerisms and regimes before negotiating:

General Mannerisms
- Proper greetings
- Dining decorum
- Rituals
- Taboos
- Values

Business Mannerisms
- Proper greetings
- Meeting etiquette
- Proper correspondences
- Negotiating decorum, strategies, and tactics
- Motivating factors

Country Regimes
- Political Stability
- Government and Local Taxes
- Government Laws and Regulations
- Natural Resources Taxes
- Percentage of Royalty Paid to the other Company and Government
- Import and Export Taxes
- Security Cost (Strikes, kidnapping, riots, acts of wars, and etc.)
- Financial Liabilities due to Legal or Contractual Issues
- Environmental Laws
- Delay of Payment
- Exchange Control, Convertibility of Currency

Copyright © 2008 Dana L. Cradeur
www.Danaiconsulting.com